Godot At Night

Books by Nathaniel Hutner

Heracleitus Under Water 1988

War: A Book Of Poems 2003

The Name We Never Lose 2019

The Complete Poems of Nathaniel Hutner 2021

※

Plays by Nathaniel Hutner

Godot Arrives

Godot Imagine Godot

Godot at Night

Godot, Alive or Dead

The President Pardons Godot

※

Short Plays by Nathaniel Hutner

Hot Potatoes

The Fix

Keewaydin Plays

Godot At Night

೫

A Comedy by Nathaniel Hutner

Burlington, Vermont

A collected edition of Nathaniel Hutner's plays, *The Collected Plays of Nathaniel Hutner*, is available from Onion River Press, 191 Bank Street, Burlington, VT 05401

Copyright © 2021 by Nathaniel Hutner

All rights reserved. No part of this publication may be reproduced, distributed, or transmitted in any form or by any means, including photocopying, recording, or other electronic or mechanical methods, without the prior written permission of the publisher, except in the case of brief quotations embodied in critical reviews and certain other noncommercial uses permitted by copyright law.

Onion River Press
191 Bank Street
Burlington, VT 05401

ISBN: 978-1-949066-89-0

Library of Congress Control Number: 2021913785

Designed by Jenny Lyons, Middlebury VT

Godot At Night

CAST OF CHARACTERS

FATHER ANSELM: A monk, about 40

GODOT

DANIEL: Adopted son of A & B

A & B: The two forgotten Apostles

MISS PRIMP: Fiancée of Professor Fish

MISS LUST: Educator

PROFESSOR FISH: Retired Academic

TOFF 1: Spouse of Toff 2

TOFF 2: Spouse of Toff 1

DR. GODOT: Psychiatrist and remote cousin of Godot

TOPS: Assistant to Miss Lust

POZZO & LUCKY: Politically ambitious deadbeats

MR. PEUCH (LATER PEACH): Merger Specialist

WAITER

ACT I

SCENE 1

    A
I figured Godot would bring rain, but not the deluge.

    B
Has it been forty days and forty nights?

    A
More.

    B
History is overtaking us.

    A
We shall have to add a new chapter to the Pentateuch.

    B
More.

    A
In the beginning, there was a beginning –

    B
And a middle –

    A
And an end.
(A farts)

    B
Save that for the end.

    A
There is one end, but many beginnings.

    B
I am feeling sick to my stomach.

    A
You are a wonder and a joy. Does my presence help alleviate the pain?

    B
Without you I would be nowhere.

    A
Yes. It is hard to put pain in its place.

    B
I don't remember – why are we here?

    A
Our enterprise failed.

    B
Pozzo and Lucky?

    A
They cooked the books and decamped with the cash.

    B
And our livelihood.

    A
So much for day-laborers.

    B
So much for the desk-executive.

    A
We'll survive.

B
We'll see. And Daniel?

  A
You don't remember?
(B is silent in his anguish)
Daniel died
(B is still silent)

  A
(Continued)
He collaborated with Pozzo and Lucky. They killed him and dressed it up as a suicide. I believe if we visit a certain meat-packing plant…
(They both break down)
(MISS LUST appears)

  MISS LUST
(To herself)
Job suffered less than these two.
(We see tears on her cheeks)
They have lost their one son; and for them, he was the wealth of the world. Tragedy herself is not so cruel.

  B
Ah, Aphrodite!
(Still choked up)

  MISS LUST
I give you my heart.

  B
Too late.
(Pause)

  A
To everything there is an end. Even misery must end.

    B
I hope death lives up to its reputation.

    MISS LUST
What has become of Godot?

    A
He's on holiday.

    MISS LUST
He died again?

    A
Yes, several times. He abandoned his identity, and without it he was nothing.

    B
How long do we have to wait this time? I am tired of waiting.

    A
I think this time he is waiting for us.

    B
Where?

    A
I think on the other side of life.

    B
Good heavens.
(Pause. A looks at B)

    A
It seems we have all failed to redeem ourselves.

    MISS LUST
Nonsense. You have simply been victimized.

    B
Well, I am prepared to act.
(Surprise)

    A
What do you propose?

    B
My old stand-by: suicide.

    MISS LUST
I am not ready. I mean, I have so many more people to help.

    A
Up to you.

    B
Ready?

    A
Ready.
(A and B kill themselves – the manner of death is left up to those involved)

    MISS LUST
I wish I inspired such devotion… I might as well try it myself. I have had enough love, and without love, I am free to be responsible.
(MISS LUST kills herself)

    PROF. FISH
(Entering, sees bodies)
Oh! A and B; and Miss Lust! Dead! A threesome! What on earth shall we do without Miss Lust? She is irreplaceable.

    MISS PRIMP
(Arriving)
I shall miss A and B much more. They were faithful – even to themselves.

    PROF. FISH
Well, they have all finally arrived.
(Ghosts of A and B appear)

      A
We don't seem to be very much mourned.

      B
I hope there is someone besides us at our funeral.

      A
We are not Winston Churchill.

      B
Thank you.

      A
We may have been simple, but we were not ordinary.

      B
We had our beguiling moments.

      A
Sustenance is no longer in doubt.

      B
We are even free to fly.
(They float up a bit and wiggle their wings – newly visible)

      A
We need practice

      B
I never thought my role in the afterlife would be to impersonate Peter Pan.

      A
Look, they cannot see or hear us!

      B
Just as well. Primp was a pill.

      A
And Fish, even in Nature, was a bit of a ding-a-ling. Now that we are translated, I wonder if we can find Daniel.

(A and B wander offstage)
(DR. GODOT enters)

   MISS PRIMP
Death is not very attractive, at least this side of it.

   DR. GODOT
It was not meant to be.

   MISS PRIMP
I wonder why?

   DR. GODOT
It beats me.

   MISS PRIMP
Perhaps it's because death is the door to bliss. Every major religion, except the Hindus, acts as though the opposite were true.

   DR. GODOT
We wouldn't want everyone to know, if it were true. It would become fashionable.

   MISS PRIMP
Right: humanity requires an education, and acquaintance with as much pain as possible. Once that is done, and the memory of it firmly engraved upon the brain, then we can proceed to Paradise and enjoy ourselves. Pain will be only a memory, and memory will be a preventative.

   DR. GODOT
I'm sold.
(They kill themselves)
(Enter TOFF 1 and TOFF 2)

   TOFF 1
A massacre!

TOFF 2
They are not fools.

TOFF 1
Reminds me of a board meeting I once attended. Is suicide really the next fashion?

TOFF 2
If so, I hope it lasts.

TOFF 1
I have always been curious…

TOFF 2
Me, too.

TOFF 1
Shall we?
(They kill themselves)
(PROFESSOR FISH and MR. TOPS enter)

PROF. FISH
Ah, the ultimate cure.

TOPS
Let us hope so. I am tired of cures.

PROF. FISH
There will be no one left.

TOPS
No one to screw.

PROF. FISH
No one to love.

TOPS
No friends, no enemies.
(They exchange glances)

               TOPS
(Continued)
   Then, at last, the world —
               PROF. FISH
   — will be at Peace.
               TOPS
   The fish will ponder their subaqueous guilt.
               PROF. FISH
   And the trout will grow thick as thorns.
               TOPS
   The hummingbird will be able to hear its own tune.
               PROF. FISH
   Enough. Let us do Mother Nature a favor.
(They kill themselves)
(POZZO and LUCKY enter)
               POZZO
   We escaped.
               LUCKY
   At last.
               POZZO
   Damnation!
               LUCKY
   What?
               POZZO
   There is no one left for us to tyrannize over.
               LUCKY
   We have money.
               POZZO
   What do we spend it on? Coffins?

LUCKY
But money can buy you anything. Love, sex, an altered face, an altered name, whole caravans of sweets from the East, pornography, psychoanalysis, speech-writers, political office, paintings by the famous, paintings of the famous, fame, even a Greek Temple for a tomb. We should be happy. Now everything belongs to us.

POZZO
Sit, slave.
(LUCKY trembles and sits)
(LUCKY is once more mute)
(Out come the ropes, only this time there are two)

POZZO
Forward, cur!
(They gradually move offstage)
(BLACKOUT)

SCENE 2 – HEAVEN

    A
Well. Our suffering is finally paying off.

    B
This chocolate shake is exquisite.

    A
And there's a choice: we can have strawberry as well.

    B
Variety beats tedium. Have you noticed, I'm not such a crab any more.

    A
You are well rid of life, so let's not dwell on it

    B
Do you think we may run into Godot here?

    DR. GODOT
Here I am!

    A
Oh. The relative.

    B
I thought you might have ended up in the downstairs department.

    DR. GODOT
Oh, no. Everyone comes here. Even those who love life.

    A
But they never suffered.

DR. GODOT
That was not their fault.

A
Oh.

B
You mean we sat around for two thousand years of pain and some twerp who lucked out in life gets the same reward?

A
I think we had better discuss this with Mr. Godot. I may ask for a refund, or a replay, or whatever.

B
Well, I'm happy to be here. Let us make the most of our opportunity.

DR. GODOT
But it isn't exclusive.

B
I don't think that's quite the right response.

DR. GODOT
Oh?

B
No. There is no such thing as social rank here. We are all dead. Why should we continue to torture each other? That is what life is for. You go through life to get it out of your system. Perhaps you should return and work on it some more.

DR. GODOT
Return?

B
Yes. It can be arranged.

DR. GODOT
I think I prefer death to life.

B
Good. Then don't muck it up.

A
Or you may find yourself reincarnated as an ass.
(DR. GODOT wilts)

A
(Continued)
Death has its rules, you know.

DR. GODOT
How do I find out what they are?

B
By breaking them.

A
It's quite a responsibility.

B
But you're up to it.
(MISS LUST enters)

A
Oh, Miss Lust – you don't look like a tart anymore.

MISS LUST
Not here. There is no sex allowed. And love is out the window. Here we do not live for pleasure, or pain, as the case may be. We are generous with our time, and enjoy each other's company. The variety of angelic types is staggering Everyone has a history. It is amazing. And they actually talk about their histories.

A
In life, that was something to avoid.

MISS LUST
Here there is nothing left for them to lose.

B
I am beginning to wonder whether life had any attractions at all.

 A
I think we were getting strung along.

 MISS LUST
Well, death seems adequate – even the blue haired ladies are amusing themselves. You should see their hair-do's: straight out of 1955.

 B
I love it.

 MISS LUST
Not only that, the supply of new angels, each with a fresh new history, is inexhaustible. I was sure that procreation had a purpose, and now I know what it was: to make angels!

 A
And we were so afraid of death.

 MISS LUST
With good cause. There is no sex in heaven, and if there is no sex in heaven, there has to be sex on earth. Otherwise, we would sooner or later run out of things to say to one another, and there would be no new angels to supply the deficiency. In fact, without life, there would be no one in heaven at all –

 B
– except Godot.

 ALL
Ahh!

 DR. GODOT
And love keeps the whole machine in gear.

MISS LUST
It is Mr. Godot who has set it all up.

A
Daniel!

DANIEL
Hooray for Godot! He told me you had arrived.

B
Yes. Here, everyone has arrived, even the aristocrats.

A
We must take care –

MISS LUST
Of anyone who happens along. It is a good way to make new and lasting friends.

B
You're the expert.

MISS LUST
(Smiles happily)
Thank you!

B
(Smiles back)
You see: here a barb has no point.

A
Are they available for export?

B
Barbs?

DANIEL
Shall we try business again?

B
I prefer listening to Rimsky-Korsakov.

DANIEL
He is certainly pleasant to know. I ran into him on the way over. Of course, I had no idea who he was, until I asked. He was very civilized, without being blasé. And he has a very handsome beard.

A
Do you think we might run into Shakespeare?

DANIEL
I asked Rimsky-Korsakov about that. He says Shakespeare is very much in demand. And the bard is more closely related to Godot than our Doctor here. If you are really keen, I think I could arrange a meeting, but you would have to hold up your end of the conversation.

A
(Looking less interested)
Well, I don't suppose I should intrude...

B
It can wait.
(Looking at A)

MISS LUST
Someone's missing.

DANIEL
Pozzo and Lucky.

DR. GODOT
They've decided to take over the world. In fact, they have taken over the world.

A
I feel sorry for the world.
(General silence)

DANIEL
I don't suppose…

B
Oh, no. Just when we begin to unwind.

DANIEL
If we go back, we can unwind there too.

A
What's the point?

DANIEL
We are only sacrificing a part of eternity to turn the world around.

DR. GODOT
Who asked you?

A
It's the uninvited guest who does the good deed, and it's a good deed because the one who does it is disinterested.

B
Why don't you have your head examined. Surely you're dumber than you look.

DANIEL
Well. Shall we?
(Everyone nods yes, some grudgingly)
(BLACKOUT)

SCENE 3

Lights up. It is early afternoon near the Outer Hebrides. The apple tree has been replaced by a blue spruce. It is decorated for Christmas. Otherwise, the landscape is what it was in Scene 1.

A
I was a working class baby.

B
We all work.

A
We just have different wardrobes.

B
And some of us try to find out our family trees.

DANIEL
You're welcome to yours. I prefer looking ahead to looking behind.

A
Looking behind cannot guarantee good behavior.

B
Or good taste.

A
Or success in life.

DANIEL
There are no guarantees.

A
It does help if you try to find out what's the case and stick to it.

DANIEL
That can be a pain.

                B
Have you tried the opposite?
(General silence)

                A
Aloha!

        MISS LUST
Me again. I have the odd feeling I've been somewhere, but where, I do not know.

                A
Me, too
(Everyone agrees)

        MISS LUST
Well, memory is fallible, and probably just as well. If we remembered even the important things, we might save ourselves.

                A
I like waiting.

        MISS LUST
It certainly doesn't require much effort.

        DANIEL
And you're waiting –

                A
– for Godot.

                B
I'm beginning to detect the familiar.

        MISS LUST
Wait! My memory! It has come back! We were in heaven, and we have returned to earth –

> A

– to be useful.

> B

Lord.

> DANIEL

Alleluia.

> A

Pozzo!
(Who is entering)
And Lucky!
(Ditto)

> B

Shall we tell them?

> DANIEL

Is the truth serviceable?

> A

They'd never believe a word.

> B

They never did.

> MISS LUST

They are out of practice when it comes to the truth. In fact, they each have only half a personality, the dark half.

> A

I always thought they were amoral.

> B

Truth for them is an enigma.

> A

Wrapped in plastic

DANIEL
Covered in –

B
Manure.

A
Let us leave them thinking so – for the time being.

B
Now what?
(A whispers to B. They all leave, except for POZZO and LUCKY)

POZZO
(Muttering to himself)
Domination without vanity is getting awfully dull. You! Lucky! Stand!
(LUCKY complies)

POZZO
(Continued)
It's always the same thing. And we're the only two here. I can't even have a decent conversation, and I've been lying to myself for years. There is no comfort in that. What if I can no longer talk to myself? Talk about solitude! Stand! Lucky! Stand!
(LUCKY stands. He has been wilting while POZZO delivers his monologue)

POZZO
(Continued)
I seem to have fallen into a pit.
(LUCKY falls over. POZZO doesn't notice)

POZZO
(Continued)
My mind is dark – it always was – I have no heart – never did – I have sold my soul, not even to the highest bidder – I was being sly, to cover my desire – money is no good, I already own

everything – and I belong to no one. I can't even die. Not that I want to. Death does not attract me – only life – of a kind – I make life hell for Lucky – that is why I call him Lucky – it is a joke.

(He groans)

(LUCKY begins to make noises with his mouth which slowly bring POZZO to a blind rage)

    POZZO

(Continued)

Beast! Turd! Beggar! Slave! Oh, my head, my head. I cannot bear to be alive. I am afraid of death. I bring death to life. The moon is in eclipse – Juno Queen of Heaven would not see me if she tried. Things are heating up. My life lies. I lie. I am half the world and I lie.

(He falls down and begins to have convulsions)

Lord, the devil is breaking my bones! This is agony!

(After a while, the fit subsides, and POZZO falls asleep)

(Meanwhile, LUCKY wakes up, takes off his ropes and quietly decamps)

(Enter A and B)

    A

He seems to be sleeping.

    B

He needs it.

    A

Did you hear him howling?

    B

Indeed.

    A

Was it his soul?

> B

I think his feet hurt.

> A

Well, I was beginning to think he didn't have a soul.

> B

Everyone has one who wants one.

> A

Is he going to wake up?

> B

Yes. After what to his sleeping soul seems like an eternity of pain.

> A

Which is for us only thirty minutes.

> B

That's a good trick.

> A

One of our better ploys. It's called "a fold in time saves nine."

> B

Do you dream?

> A

All the time. It's my specialty.

> B

Well, I approve of the results.

> A

Thank you.

> B

You said thirty minutes?

> A

Time is collapsible. Your patience is too. Ready?

(POZZO stands up, but is still asleep. He is sleep-walking)

        A

Pozzo!

(POZZO turns to A)

        A

Tell us what you love!

       POZZO

Nobody.

        A

And what do you possess?

       POZZO

Nothing.

        A

Who are you?

       POZZO

Nobody.

        A

What are you?

       POZZO

Nothing.

        A

How do you see?

       POZZO

I see nothing.

        A

Where do you feel?

       POZZO

Nowhere.

             B
Pozzo, is this what you want?
(POZZO says nothing)
(Pause)

             B
(Continued)
Pozzo, do you want nothing?

          POZZO
I want everything.
(Pause)

             A
Everything is nothing
(BLACKOUT)

SCENE 4

Lights up. Tea time. GODOT is having tea with A and B.

GODOT
So you see, that is my dilemma. Pozzo was quite accurate – along with you, A. Everything is infinite – and everything is therefore nothing. Reality requires boundaries, just as sense – or language – requires rules. Without rules there is chaos and without boundaries there is nothing. My problem now is that the boundaries are breaking down. We must find a way to build them back up, or the universe is lost.

A
Milk or lemon?

GODOT
Milk, please, with two sugars.

B
What can we do?

GODOT
Quite simple. This all happened because I was dead – by choice. In the interim the universe was handed over to the forces of darkness – and remains there except for this earth.

A
We are the last refuge of the light?

GODOT
Yes, with a little bit of cleaning. You are very inconspicuous, and for the moment you remain overlooked. Soon enough that will not be the case. And I have taken the trouble to tell you so. You ought to be prepared to defend yourselves, and then the rest of creation as well.

> B

That's a bit stiff.

> A

Ready for Star Wars?

> GODOT

The threat is already present.

> A

What do you do with a threatening presence?

> GODOT

First, you talk to them; then you take the threat out of their hands; then you talk some more.

> A

It's called disarming the threatening presence?

> GODOT

Yes.

> B

It seems to work.

> GODOT

Yes.

> B

So far.

> A

If we spend our time as peace-makers, how do we support ourselves?

> B

The last carrot is gone.

> A

No more rutabaga.

GODOT
You both are invited to earn a handsome salary as managers.

A
Managers are generally paid more for their services than the common man.

GODOT
That is because their responsibilities are greater. Their failures affect their colleagues, their superiors and their subordinates. If the common man fails, it is he alone who suffers.

B
And his family.

A
If he has one.

B
That is why some people avoid the upper crust: it is a risky place, and one is constantly in danger of being held up.

A
Or celebrated.

A
Same thing.

GODOT
I shall try to make your profile quite flat.

A
Thank you.

B
Well.
(LUCKY appears, well-dressed and nicely groomed)
(He putters about)

A
What about Pozzo and Lucky?

    B
Those who rule the world must learn to rule themselves.

    A
And we're their learning material?

    GODOT
Yes.

    B
Then we are making them a gift of ourselves.

    A
But that is all we have.

    GODOT
Yes.

    B
You will find that they do not realize what they have.

    GODOT
Until it is no longer theirs.

    A
And then it is too late.

    B
Yes.

    A
At which point they are reduced to nothing.

    GODOT
That is how things are arranged.

(BLACKOUT)

SCENE 5

(A and B enter)

      A
Life sometimes limps.

      B
Tell me.

      A
Let's go back to heaven! Things there were certain.

      B
Up to you.
(They remain fixed to the spot)

      A
Seems to me I've done this before.

      B
Out of different motives.
(They smile)
(MISS LUST enters)

      A
Miss Lust, how are you?

      MISS LUST
Travelin'. It's so fatiguin'.

      A
By train?

      MISS LUST
No. Foot.

      A
Any customers?

MISS LUST
We are ghosts.

A
I forgot. But now that we are here, everything is back to where it was. What is that on your nose?

MISS LUST
Oh, a bit of –

A
Take my handkerchief.
(MISS LUST breaks down)

MISS LUST
It is so difficult to be dead here. In heaven I was happy. Here I am constantly confronted with my past. It is so hard to see what you were, it reminds you of what you might have become. I would like to move on.

B
(To A)
She's in fine shape.

A
At least she knows where she fits in.

B
We may find her something to do here.

A
Something useful.

B
Besides sex.

A
She may need retraining.

B
That is all right. Miss Lust!

MISS LUST
Yes?

B
Come with us. We think we may cook up something for you to do: something fun.

MISS LUST
Really?
(They all exit)

SCENE 6

    A
We must respect our feelings – they are guides to ourselves, and to others.

    B
Some people do not relish their feelings.

    A
Some people do not relish the feelings of others.

    B
The subject is inexhaustible.

    A
I don't think so.

    B
I hope you're right.

    A
I knew someone once who deliberately set himself up all the time.

    B
Yes, and then he got knocked down. It was edifying.

    A
And then he got back on his feet –

    B
– and did it again.

    A
It was Godot. In his youth.

B
Did we know him then?

A
I don't know.

B
Why did he do it?

A
He wanted to be human.
(B shakes his head)

A
Are we human?

B
I think we have graduated.

A
Thank goodness.

B
Of course, if you're alone, there's no one to knock you down.

A
Yes.

B
Are we alone?

A
You are here with me.

B
You are here with me.

A
I have always trusted you.

B
It's mutual.

A
You have never failed me, even when sex was in question.

B
Sex is not everything.

A
Mr. Tops helped most graphically.

B
I was not jealous.

A
No, you were an angel. You understood my problem.

B
You understood mine.

A
I love you. I love you more than I deserve.

B
Me, too.

A
How long will all this last?

B
I guess Godot has the answer to that: until we get tired of it.

A
Then let's take our time.

B
I shall follow you beyond imagination.

A
Perhaps we should get married.

B
That is beyond imagination.

A
It is nothing, when you are contemplating the end of time.

B
Well, let's stick it out here for a few more years and see how we feel then.

A
You were always cautious.

B
We have done quite well so far without ceremony. Why mess it all up?

A
You're a genius.

B
I try to be sensible.

A
Did you ever feel guilty about the sex act?

B
No. It was an expression of my love. Why should I feel guilty about love?

(Silence)

B
(Continued)
That is why I cannot enjoy one-night stands.

A
There is no love.

B
I require warm-ups, dinner parties, book-fairs, bicycling, even TV. I do not treat love lightly.

A
Love does not treat us lightly.

B
Just so.

A
Think of it. I have been loving you in so many ways for 2001 years, and I didn't know it.

B
I did.

A
I always get nervous when people start telling each other how much they love one another.

B
People talk a lot.

A
I never cared for gossip.

B
Me neither. It is tinsel.

A
Dressed in words.

B
It is often fatal.

A
It has destroyed many good people.

B
Godot was a good person.

A
I thought he was just acting.

B
If so, it was because acting was his life.

A

Some acts are hard to comprehend.

B

We must try to see clearly.

A

We are not Gods.

B

No. But we needn't all be fools.

A

Do you know what comes next?

B

More love?

A

Heavens preserve us.

B

Yes. Heaven. That's it.

A

But we were there just a short time ago.

B

Let's follow the Little Prince and go back.

A

It's less trouble.

B

I don't think we are really welcome here.

A

No one talks to us.

B

They don't let us know that they are thinking of us.

    A
Yes they do.

    B
You're right, I am wrong – they do show some care.

    A
Some people are very solicitous.

    B
I suppose we should stay and encourage the trend.

    A
It would help.

    B
I don't know anybody's name.

    A
It would help to ask: you would simply be showing your interest. It would be a compliment.

    B
Are we interested?

    A
Let us try it out for a few years.

    B
We are free to leave at any time.

    A
Yes. That is how things are arranged.
(BLACKOUT)

SCENE 7

TOFF 2
Well, Miss Lust, are you prepared to surprise us?

MISS LUST
Excuse me?

TOFF 2
We have all been invited to Mr. Puech's for a party.

MISS LUST
Who is Mr. Puech?

TOFF 2
You will see when you meet him.

MISS LUST
His picture makes him look a little crazed.

TOFF 2
He is a busy man.

MISS LUST
I am a busy woman.

TOFF 1
Try him on for size.

MISS LUST
I am not coming out of retirement for anyone, least of all Mr. Puech. What an ugly name.

TOFF 1
I will keep an eye out for you.

MISS LUST
Are you proposing a pecuniary emolument?

TOFF 1

Well…

MISS LUST

I would sooner be the Hermit on the Mount than sell myself. My self is all I have. Everyone seems to like money. It is like a disease, an infectious disease. I prefer not to go to extremes, even with money.

TOFF 1

It is best to be comfortable without extravagance.

TOFF 2

I am comfortable without anything.

TOFF 1

That helps.

TOFF 2

Not everyone born into the upper middle class ends up writing poetry for nothing.

MISS LUST

You need a sideline.

TOFF 2

You, my dear.

MISS LUST

What?

TOFF 2

We make a striking pair. If we get the right invitations, we can live off the fat of the land.

MISS LUST

You mean crumbs from above.

TOFF 2

Mr. Puech seems to be willing to give us some practice. In

return, I shall dedicate my next poem to him. I think he will be pleased.

 TOFF 1
Well, are you ready?

 TOFF 2
Yes.

 MISS LUST
I need to practice.

 TOFF 2
Wing it, dear. They'll love you in any case.

 MISS LUST
Oh!

 TOFF 1
You can come as Glinda the Good.

 TOFF 2
I shall be the Muse of Poetry.

 TOFF 1
I shall be the Oracle of Delphi.

 MISS LUST
I always wanted my future told.

 TOFF 1
I shall try.

 TOFF 2
You can practice on tea-leaves.

 MISS LUST
Oh!

 TOFF 2
If you need help, I'll be watching.

MISS LUST
Thank you.

TOFF 1
Remember: courage.

TOFF 2
I'll pick you up if you fall down.

MISS LUST
Ready.
(They all exit together)

SCENE 8

MISS LUST
But I do not want your money, Mr. Puech. I cannot sell myself into slavery.

MR. PUECH
We are all free to be slaves, Miss Lust. And I offer you the most attractive opportunity.

MISS LUST
Your money is worth nothing, Mr. Puech, and so are you.

MR. PUECH
(Momentarily silent, then produces a large wad of bills and says)
    I have further reserves.
(MISS LUST turns her back on PUECH and goes as far away from him as she can)
(TOFF 1 and TOFF 2 enter)

TOFF 1
Ah. Perhaps we should withdraw.

TOFF 2
We always get our timing wrong.

TOFF 1
(Looking lovingly at TOFF 2)
    Except once.

TOFF 2
Miss Lust! You're early.

MISS LUST
I needed some warm-up.

TOFF 1
Looks like you got it.

MISS LUST
He makes propositions. It is very tiresome. I suppose he has not found out.

TOFF 2
Found out what?

MISS LUST
We are ghosts.

TOFF 2
Miss Lust, as long as we are here, we are not ghosts.

MISS LUST
What about A and B? They van disappear at will.

TOFF I
They are a special case. They have earned a little cream on their cake.

MISS LUST
Then I shall need some money.
(She looks for PUECH)

TOFF 2
Only enough to live on, with something thrown in for lollipops.

MISS LUST
Thanks. Who's the sugar daddy?

TOFF 1
Daniel. He's been working his tail off for us all.
(MISS LUST melts)

MISS LUST
He always was a dear. I guess he could be a pupil. I owe it to him.

            TOFF 2
Careful.
            MISS LUST
Ok.
(Enter A and B)
            A
A morgue.
            B
Madame Tussaud's.
            A
Parliament.
            B
Wherever.
            A
Are you being persnickety?
            B
What?
            A
Snap, snap, snap.
            B
What?
            A
Where is your hearing?
            B
What?
            A
I shall die.
            B
Yes.

   A
Oh, God.

   B
Yes.

   A
I give up.

   B
So do I.

   TOFF 1
A! B!

   A & B
Halloo!

   A
We have given up.

   TOFF 1
Don't throw your chips away. We are all about to cash them in, with Mr. Puech here.

   TOFF 2
Wealth is transient.

   B
So is life, but I don't cash it in.

   A
You can cash in anything.
(B pulls out a gnawed rutabaga from his pocket)
(Everyone looks at the rutabaga)

   B
You must be right.

   TOFF 2
Save it. You may need it.

A

Good idea. Look; here come Fish and Miss Primp.
(PROF. FISH and MISS PRIMP enter)

PROF. FISH

Delighted.
(He shakes hands all round)

MISS PRIMP

Delighted.
(She shakes hands, etc.)

A

Still fishing, Professor?

PROF. FISH

For trout, yes. Metaphorically speaking, no. It is too much for a man my age. The trout bite, but my feet freeze.

MISS PRIMP

You can always warm them, dear.

PROF. FISH

Yes, we are engaged to be married.

B

What a generous gesture.

A

Do not make fun of hope, nor of gestures.

B

Hope is not exactly a hot number.

A

We have already established there are no guarantees. Do you wish to change our minds?

B

No.

PROF. FISH
We are happy.

MISS PRIMP
Yes.

A
You have our sincere good wishes.

PROF. FISH
Thank you.

A
We need something to drink.

MISS PRIMP
Allow me.
(A WAITER goes by and she orders drinks)
(Re-enter WAITER followed by MISS LUST)

WAITER
(To MISS PRIMP)
Ma'am.

MISS PRIMP
Thank you.
(WAITER serves other drinks)

MISS LUST
(Eyeing WAITER)
If only I were back in business.

MR. PUECH
Ah! Miss Lust.
(PUECH places his hand on MISS LUST's derriere – and then finds he can't get it off)

MISS LUST
Mr. Puech! You are being naughty.
(PUECH's hand is still stuck to MISS LUST's bottom)

MISS LUST
(Continued)
Well!
(She moves away, dragging PUECH with her)
Are you deaf?

MR. PUECH
It is not my fault.

MISS LUST
It most certainly is. Ouch!

MR. PUECH
Ouch!

MISS LUST
You are too fresh! I should go back into business just to give you a lesson. Ouch!

MR. PUECH
Miss Lust…

MISS LUST
Creep!
(She starts swatting PUECH with her purse)

MR. PUECH
Ouch! Oh!

MISS LUST
I need a drink. Mr. Puech, don't try to buy me off. I know your type: you are a grab-snatcher. Well snatch someone else's grab – or grab someone else's snatch. I will not be violated by a drunken plutocrat. You are all the same. You think that because you have money, the world is yours. Well it isn't. One red rose, even with thorns, is worth ten Puechs, or a hundred. Ouch! Stop that! You should be committed. Oh! Ouch!

MR. PUECH
It's not my fault. I just meant..

MISS LUST
You didn't mean anything. You never do. Your life has no meaning. It begins and ends with dollar signs. The sun at dawn is my witness: you live a lie. You are a monomaniac, at the very least. And women, for you, are toys, pleasant but expendable. Well, I am not available, nor expendable. And you cannot have me, however attached you are. So take your filthy hand somewhere else. You may have earned money, but you have not earned me.
(She takes a swipe at PUECH and his hand comes free)
Ah!

MR. PUECH
(Weary)
That was hell.

MISS LUST
Some people's heaven can turn out that way.

B
(To PUECH)
Perhaps you should stick to finance.

MR. PUECH
This is my house, not yours. I'll not be laughed at.

A
Mr. Puech, ridicule is better than hypocrisy, don't you think? It clears the air and provides amusement at the same time. I know, you are not amused. I am sorry, but that is the only way to get through the serious little dramas of day-to-day existence: with a smile. There!
(PUECH smiles)

MR. PUECH
But this is my house. I own it. You are my guests.

A
You are backsliding, Mr. Puech. Try that smile again.
(PUECH tries and fails)

A
(Continued)
Well, some practice should help. Come with me.
(They retire to a corner of the room)

MISS LUST
That was too much.

B
Such devotion

TOFF 1
He was enthralled.

TOFF 2
You are a nice shape.

MISS LUST
Yes, but please don't touch.

TOFF 2
Ever think of marriage?

MISS LUST
It is rapidly becoming an attractive possibility.

TOFF 1
Where is Godot?

MISS LUST
Please. I am not that upwardly mobile.

TOFF 1
You will settle for…?

MISS LUST
None of your business. My plans are my own. So is my life.

B
Good.
(A and PUECH return to party)

A
Mr. Puech, it turns out, loves money more than Miss Lust. I have the evidence.

MISS LUST
We do not need evidence. We need trust.

MR. PUECH
I want my money.

B
There you are.
(An avalanche of dollar bills covers PUECH. His head appears after a few moments)

MR. PUECH
Oooohh.

B
That is what I like to see: a man immersed in his work.

MISS LUST
Mr. Puech, your task is to count every dollar. When you are through, you may keep it all. But, if you make a mistake, or lose your place, you must start over.

MR. PUECH
(Already counting)
3, 4, 5, 6, 7, 8, 9…

MISS LUST
Some party. I get raped and Puech gets the booby prize: and he doesn't know it.

B
He will.
(A giggles)

A
This is poetic justice.

B
What's poetic about it?

A
Ask the expert.
(He looks at TOFF 2)

TOFF 2
It is poetic because it is simultaneously metaphorical and real. Mr. Puech is a metaphor. His money is real. Or perhaps it's the other way around. Same difference.

A
But money is just paper.

B
Tell him that.

TOFF 2
He will find it out.

A
If money is just paper, what use is it?

B
It is very efficacious in the loo.

A
Oh.
(B giggles)

B
Let's blow this joint.
(Exit all but PUECH, who continues counting)

SCENE 9

PUECH is still counting his money. There are two piles of bills; on his left, the counted, on his right, the uncounted. He looks quite content and is humming to himself. MISS LUST enters.

          MISS LUST
Well, Puech, still counting?
(PUECH ignores this)

          MISS LUST
(Continued)
    Fascinating, isn't it? Like solitaire. It could go on indefinitely.
(As an afterthought)
    How old are you?
(PUECH is becoming annoyed)

          MISS LUST
(Continued)
    You know, we have said this before: money can only buy what is for sale. Mr. Puech, you have sold yourself.
(PUECH loses a beat)

          MISS LUST
(Continued)
    Ooops. You don't want to begin again. You are not young, and you have a lot of work ahead of you.
(Gesturing to the two piles, etc.)
    I never cared for accountancy. Too many numbers. They get mixed up, and then you have problems. Of course, you can blame them on someone else. Look at Pozzo. Look at Lucky. Humanity is, I suppose, not to blame. You, Mr. Puech, are working alone. So all the responsibility is yours. Very courageous of you. I would not do it, even if I could count. But

I do not count, so I don't.
(PUECH loses his count)

          MR. PUECH
Damnation woman! Why do you talk?

          MISS LUST
All women talk, in between ironing shirts.

          MR. PUECH
You have ruined my work. I was up to 1,782.

          MISS LUST
Then go on to 1,783.

          MR. PUECH
Oh. Thank you.

          MISS LUST
I try to help.

          MR. PUECH
But I know I lost a few, listening to you.

          MISS LUST
You could begin again.

          MR. PUECH
This is too much.

          MISS LUST
Of course it is.
(PUECH looks very unhappy)

          MISS LUST
(Continued)
You are used to having some one do it for you.
(PUECH looks disconsolate)

          MISS LUST
(Continued)

Now you are stuck with the grind. But it has taught you something, hasn't it?

    MR. PUECH

I hate it.

    MISS LUST

What do you hate?

    MR. PUECH

(After a long pause)

I hate money. It has destroyed my life.

    MISS LUST

Look at A and B – they never had money, and they survived.

    MR. PUECH

We seem to live at the extremes.

    MISS LUST

Bravo. And –

    MR. PUECH

I am lost.

    MISS LUST

Only your money is lost, Mr. Puech. You are still here.

(PUECH looks around, brightens)

    MR. PUECH

You mean I don't need this money?

    MISS LUST

Of course not. There are many other ways to live, most of them healthy. Take your pick. You will have enough to live on.

    MR. PUECH

I like roses.

    MISS LUST

So do I. What is your favorite color?

MR. PUECH
Red – but I really like almost all colors equally.

MISS LUST
Red. That is the color of love.
(PUECH tunes in)

MISS LUST
(Continued)
Yes. You are right on target, Mr. Puech, with red roses.

MR. PUECH
What do you want me to do?

MISS LUST
What do you want to do, Mr. Puech? That is the question.

MR. PUECH
My house has a garden. And there are many roses. And some of them are red.

MISS LUST
You are a genius, Mr. Puech. Do you know what a garden is for?

MR. PUECH
To live in.

MISS LUST
Hoorah!
(PUECH begins to cry)
(MISS LUST joins in)

MISS LUST
Our world is a garden. It was once beautiful.

MR. PUECH
It will be beautiful again.

MISS LUST
(Wiping away a few tears)
Truth always moves me, Mr. Puech. You too, I see. Well, what about the roses?

MR. PUECH
To work!

MISS LUST
To work!

MR. PUECH
To the gift of our garden.

MISS LUST
Let us move forward –

MR. PUECH
– And undo the past.

MISS LUST
Let us explore the unexplored.

MR. PUECH
And be happy at home.

MISS LUST
Mr. Puech, you are a wonder.

MR. PUECH
Miss Lust, the world is a wonder, and we are in it.
(They join hands, do a little dance, and then exit toward the garden)
(BLACKOUT)

SCENE 10

    A
What are we doing?

    B
Are we doing something? In the dark?

    A
I am breathing.

    B
You could stop.

    A
It doesn't work. I tried.

    B
Ah, life.

    A
Is there a light?
(Lights up. They are in PUECH's garden)

    B
I thought I smelled something.

    A
Oooh. Roses.

    B
It is a jungle.

    A
We could help prune.

    B
I thought Puech was counting dollars.

>A

Me, too.

>B

He has become a gardener.

>A

In the closet.

>B

Nonsense. Being a gardener is no reason for shame.

>A

Are we ashamed?

>B

Are we alive?

>A

This garden needs help.

>B

Where is Puech?

(PUECH's head appears from a mass of blooms)

>MR. PUECH

Ah, visitors! We are not ready for visitors, but you are welcome, anyway.

>A

Thank you.

(B nods)

>A

(Continued)

Do you need help?

>MR. PUECH

Well, not really. It will take time. It may take a lifetime. But I am patient.

A

You are also determined.

B

This must be a new world for you, Mr. Puech.
(PUECH smiles)

A

Do you think we could re-anoint you? Why not pronounce your name peach?
(PEACH beams)

A

Good.

B

Well, Mr. Peach, welcome to the world. It has been our garden for 2001 years, more or less. We went where we could –

A

And ended up on a stony promontory near the Outer Hebrides.

B

We were safe from the world.

A

The world was safe from us.

B

There were no roses. But we had visitors, even near the Outer Hebrides.

A

And now we have a garden to visit: with roses.

B

It is too much.

A

And you, Mr. Peach. I can see you have made several correct choices.

(PEACH blushes)

    A

(Continued)

And you are just beginning to appreciate the results.

(PEACH nods)

    MR. PEACH

There will be time –

    A

To prepare a face –

    B

To meet the faces that you meet…

    A

You are on the right road, Mr. Peach.

    B

Don't let the tricky parts throw you, Mr. Peach.

    MR. PEACH

They already have.

    A

Then you are prepared.

    MR. PEACH

You got it.

    A

Mr. Peach, you are on the right road. We must all, sooner or later, go to school.

    B

And school is not a building.

    MR. PEACH

It is a state of mind.

            A
Oooh, I love it,

            MR. PEACH
It is a capacity.

            A
Is comedy allowed?

            MR. PEACH
Without question. It was comedy that moved me.
(A and B smile broadly)

            B
You may have felt uncomfortable –

            A
(With a smile)
   You survived.
(BLACKOUT)

SCENE 11

GODOT is alone onstage as the lights go up. GODOT swats at fly.

GODOT
This place ought to be debugged.
(Enter POZZO, tied to a chain. LUCKY follows, directing POZZO)

LUCKY
Right, left. Left. Right. Stop!

POZZO
Bugs? It is just Mother Nature. Birds live on bugs.

LUCKY
Barn swallows.

GODOT
What?

POZZO
Barn swallows live on bugs. If you carry things far enough in the food chain, we live on barn swallows.

GODOT
Oh.
(Pause)
How are the politicians?

POZZO
We are thriving.

GODOT
You have changed roles.

POZZO
Hardly.

> LUCKY
He lost the election.

> GODOT
But there are only two of you.

> LUCKY
His ballot was invalidated. Non compos mentis.

> GODOT
Oh. Who figured that one out?

> POZZO
I did.

> GODOT
This is a vicious circle.

> POZZO
It is a circle, but it is not vicious.

> LUCKY
He is allowed to wash dishes.
(POZZO beams)

> LUCKY
(Continued)
Everyone is happy.
(Looks around)

> GODOT
I am glad to hear it.
(Looks around doubtfully)
(Pause)
Do you have company?
(LUCKY tries to speak, but POZZO gets there first)

> POZZO
We are each other's own best company.

LUCKY
If we get tired of one arrangement, its opposite is always possible.

POZZO
That is when we have an election.

GODOT
Oh.

POZZO
I am liberal.

LUCKY
I am conservative.

POZZO
When we get tired of that –

GODOT
You switch.

LUCKY
Yes.

GODOT
What does liberal mean?

POZZO
Whatever you want. They'll make room for you.

GODOT
And the same for conservative?

LUCKY
Just about. The liberals say the conservatives care only about themselves.

GODOT
Do they have friends?

LUCKY
Yes.

GODOT
Do they have family?

LUCKY
Yes.

GODOT
Do they have charities?

LUCKY
Yes.

GODOT
Then I cannot see that the liberals are fair with the conservatives.

LUCKY
Some conservatives are wealthy.

GODOT
I suppose some liberals are, too.

LUCKY
But they don't get picked on.

GODOT
It sounds as though the liberals are exploiting the opportunity to make their opponents feel guilty.

LUCKY
Bingo.

GODOT
Do liberals ever feel guilty?

LUCKY
All the time. It is the fault of the conservatives.

GODOT
It seems you all want to be happy, but you don't know how.

LUCKY
So.

GODOT
Why not choose new goals?

LUCKY
What?

POZZO
What?

GODOT
Well, why not be in favor of someone other than yourselves?

LUCKY
I am against abortion.

POZZO
Conservative.

LUCKY
I am in favor of free trade.

POZZO
Middle-of-the-road.

LUCKY
Hooray for the Sandanistas!

POZZO
Very liberal.

LUCKY
I –

GODOT
Enough.

POZZO
You see? One label won't do. We need several, and the chance to change over time.

LUCKY
But that is more work.

GODOT
It may provide better answers.
(General silence)

GODOT
(Continued)
By the way, I would leave room for the individual.

LUCKY
I would, too. I think we've been railroaded.

POZZO
Surprise, surprise.

LUCKY
We did it to ourselves.

POZZO
Surprise, surprise. We are not very good politicians.

LUCKY
We can think.
(Pause)
What do we do now?

GODOT
Lie low.
(LUCKY drops his rope. Chains fall from POZZO, who doesn't notice – he is lost in his lucubrations and strikes a grand pose, totally unawares. LUCKY takes his cue from POZZO. For the first

time in their history, they appear human, stately but vulnerable. Soon enough, they will trust each other. From that, everyone will take his cue)
(SLOW FADE)

SCENE 12

    A
It is very odd.

    B
What?

    A
Odd. It's peculiar.

    B
What is peculiar?

    A
That we are still here.

    B
Yes. We are the eyes of Paradise. We are beginning to be responsible.

    A
You tell that to the people and you'll get royally walloped.

    B
Am I talking?

    A
Only to me.

    B
So. Are you talking?

    A
Only to you.

    B
What about the obliquity of time?

  A
I think we should leave time to the philosophers.
  B
You can count on it, they will confuse the issue.
  A
They will confuse themselves.
  B
That is philosophy.
  A
Ouch.
  B
Your hair is full of burrs. Where have you been sleeping?
  A
By your tent.
  B
Oh. I thought we generally shared in our sleeping arrangements.
  A
I like to be alone sometimes.
  B
Oh.
  A
It allows my heart to breathe.
  B
Mine, too.
  A
Thank you.
(B smiles and pecks A's cheek)

       A
(Continued)
   I am melting again.

       B
   Save it! For tonight – in both tents; we can alternate, if you like.

       A
   I've got my eye on you, not the tents.
(B smiles again and adds a peck to the first one)

       A
   I don't think we look our age.
(Eyeing a small mirror he has pulled out of his pocket)

       B
   We look older.

       A
   Nonsense. I would say you look 40 and I look 39.

       B
   What's the difference?

       A
   You're supposed to know more than me.
(B beams but says nothing)

       A
(Continued)
   Life is not always generous.

       B
   At least we have not shriveled up into grasshoppers.

       A
   No. We are well preserved.

       B
   For what purpose?

    A
We are witnesses.

    B
You mean we see everything and report it upstairs?

    A
Yes.

    B
I hope we stay here permanently.

    A
London would overwhelm us in two seconds.

    B
I cannot overhear more than three conversations at a time.

    A
London would be impossible. Peach's party was enough.

    B
Me, too.

    A
Here we entertain one guest at a time.

    B
If they come.

    A
Yes.

    B
It teaches tolerance.

    A
And forgiveness.

    B
Where appropriate.

> A
>
> Where there is crime –
>
> B
>
> There is punishment.
>
> A
>
> In the end we all dig our own graves.
>
> B
>
> It is called life.

(They are silent for a while)

> A
>
> We do not spill the milk.
>
> B
>
> We spill the truth.
>
> A
>
> It is not a happy job sometimes.
>
> B
>
> A mess is a mess.
>
> A
>
> What did that man Goethe say?
>
> B
>
> If everyone swept his own threshold, the world would be clean.
>
> A
>
> It is, here.

(They smile at one another)

> B
>
> I wish we could help further.
>
> A
>
> We do.

B
Nobody says thank you.

A
Nobody says a thing.

B
(Shouting)
Where is everybody?
(There is an echo, then silence)
If they told me this was earth, I wouldn't believe it.

A
Why not?

B
Look.
(They do so)

A
Perhaps we're in Hell.

B
It's a possibility.

A
Why stay?

B
Ineptitude on the part of the Authorities.

A
They probably forgot we were here. It's like the Army.

B
Are we supposed to be fighting someone?

A
Ourselves.

B
Why?

A
We are expected to change our feelings?

B
No thank you.

A
We're off to a wonderful start.

B
What I have always done is all that I can think of doing.

A
Courage, yes. Imagination, no.

B
I give up.

A
Nonsense. You are on the threshold of a miracle and you crap out. Collect yourself. We're going for a ride.
(A two person bicycle appears. They get on and ride off)
(LIGHTS DIM)

SCENE 13

The Stage is bare except for a table with a telephone. The telephone begins to ring. No one appears. The telephone rings again. No one appears again. The telephone stops ringing. A and B rush in just in time to greet the silence.

    A
All that riding.

    B
Are you sure it was ringing?

    A
No. But it might have been.

    B
We will never know.

    A
It could have been Godot.

    B
With instructions.

    A
Where to meet.

    B
What to do.

    A
We already know what to do.

    B
Yes. We don't need Godot to tell us that.

        A
Our first meeting was helpful.
(Pause)

        B
Where is everybody?

        A
On a picnic.

        B
Oh.

        A
What if it was Godot? We might have missed something important.

        B
He'll call again

        A
If it was him.
(Silence)

        A
(Continued)
   We missed the picnic too?

        B
Yes, Pozzo and Lucky made the arrangements. Here they come.
(POZZO and LUCKY arrive in business suits. They look very smart)

        B
(Continued)
(Sotto voce)
   This is too much.

A
Shhh!

B
(To POZZO)
A little respite, eh?
(POZZO nods and starts picking HIS teeth)

B
(Continued)
Fine weather.
(POZZO belches)

A
Good food, Mr. Pozzo?

POZZO
Splendid.
(Pulls out menu)

POZZO
(Continued)
(To A)
Here.

A
Ohh! Cream of celery soup, quail, sherbet, Beef Wellington, salad, crepes flambees, cognac, cigars.

B
With all that to tuck into, we could survive for another 2000 years.

A
No problem.

B
How was it, Mr. Pozzo?
(POZZO belches again)

                    B
(Continued)
   That good?

                    A
Mr. Pozzo, you must try to include us all next time.
(POZZO resumes picking his teeth)

                    A
(Continued)
   Oral hygiene is very important.

                    B
But not when you don't eat. There's nothing to pick.

                    A
We have done very well at not eating.

                    B
We have enough practice.

                    A
We must have been dead.

                    B
Mr. Pozzo, does Lucky participate in your gustatory extravaganzas?
(POZZO kicks LUCKY, who has fallen asleep on the floor)

                    A
Back to square one.

                    B
How long did that take?

                    A
Two weeks.

                    B
All that hard work. All those words.

A
It kept us busy.

B
Pozzo was busy.

A
Running this place is not easy, especially when it is depopulated.

B
All the rewards are empty.

A
That's appropriate.

B
Lucky is a slave by choice.

A
We are all free to be slaves.

B
I think I've heard that already.

A
It's still true.

(POZZO and LUCKY go off. MISS LUST appears)

MISS LUST
Oh, our man of the moment is not much to gauge goodness by.

B
That is not the business of rulers. If they are young they are foolish and want everything arranged to their own taste. When they are old, they are beyond redemption, and what they do is unmentionable.

A
I can mention it.

        B
Please.

        A
(Finger to lips)
Shhh.

        B
Sometimes madness is inscrutable.

        A
Perhaps we should be cynical for a while.

        B
I'd rather be a hypocrite. It is less trouble.

        A
It's a matter of judgement and discipline. Very few people advertise what they are for all the world to know.

        B
Look at Godot.
(They both throw up their arms)
(BLACKOUT)

SCENE 14

A bathroom.

        MISS PRIMP
My bathtub is full of jello!

        LUCKY
"There's always room for jello."

        MISS PRIMP
In me, or in my bathtub?

        POZZO
Maybe I can buy my way out of this dessert.

        MISS PRIMP
(Handing POZZO a spoon)
  Eat!
(They all begin to eat jello)
(BLACKOUT)

SCENE 15

    A
Where is Miss Primp?

    B
On a picnic. She's taking care of dessert.

    A
Ooh. I love cheesecake.

    B
I hear her specialty is jello. It is easy to prepare, especially in quantity.

    A
She must be preparing for a trip to India.

    B
What is this with India?

    A
They are a former colony of the British, and inherited Socialism as their creed.

    B
Socialism – Smocialism, as long as they learn to govern.

    A
They follow the usual rules.

    B
I wasn't aware there were rules.

    A
It depends what game you want to play.
(Pause)
    There are rules.

                B
What happens if they are broken?

                A
Heads roll.

                B
Mine has always felt a bit loose.

                A
It depends how you wear it.

                B
Mine is always a bit peaked.

                A
It is not your hair.

                B
I shall talk to Miss Primp.
(He goes off)

                A
Ahh. A moment of solitude. After almost 2,000 years. This is unexpected. Ahh.
(A lies down and dozes off. PEACH enters and begins gardening. A wakes up and screams)

                A
(Continued)
   Oh! Mr. Puech.

            MR. PEACH
It is Peach, now, thank you. I have been baptized for the second time.

                A
Like a boat, revamped and retitled.

            MR. PEACH

No. With water, like a baby.

    A

You have earned it.
(PEACH is silent)
(B re-enters)

    B

Deserved what?

    A

Religion

    MR. PEACH

I was re-christened.

    B

You needed a bath. That is all.

    A

Religion is a kind of cold bath.

    B

I like mine warm.

    A

Hot or cold, it is all religion.

    B

I have given it up.

    A

There is so much to choose from: Hinduism, Buddhism, Islam, and many varieties of Christianity.

    B

They can't all be true. It would not be logically possible.

    A

Many things that are not logically possible happen anyway.

    B

Just as well. It is the impossibilities that count.

    A

I always inclined toward Heraclitus and the Tao.

    B

The Tao?

    A

Yes. It is Chinese. It multiplies its meanings as you go along.

    B

It is like poetry.

    A

Yes.

    B

Where is Toff 2?

    A

Who knows? You do not need an expert to read poetry. You need a sensibility.

    B

What good is that?

    A

It teaches us who we are.

    B

Now I know why no one reads poetry.

    A

What do we do with Peach here?

    B

Let him dig. A rose is a rose, however many you plant. I can never tire of roses.

    A

But he is planting only red roses.

        B
Perhaps he is trying to tell us something.

        A
Red is the color of love.

        B
Mr. Peach?

        MR. PEACH
At your service.

        B
Are you in love?

        MR. PEACH
I am firmly attached to red roses. It is the result of a misunderstanding.

        B
Excuse me?

        MR. PEACH
I had one rose with three thorns. By accident, I stepped on my rose at night, in the dark. And it died. I lost the one thing I cherished above all the universe. And then I came here and – surprise – found not one red rose, but hundreds, thousands even. Mother Nature is very generous here.
(Enter MISS LUST, LUCKY and POZZO)

        MISS LUST
I see roses everywhere.

        LUCKY
They are blinding in the light.

        MISS LUST
It is Mr. Peach. He is planting roses, red roses, everywhere.

LUCKY
Even in the North Country.

MISS LUST
Some roses are very hardy.

POZZO
Yes!

LUCKY
Their perfume is heavenly.

B
Appropriate.

POZZO
Should we lend a hand?

MISS LUST
No...Let Mr. Peach do the roses. We could try fruit trees. Apples, plums, pears. Whatever will flourish in the appropriate place.

(DANIEL enters)

DANIEL
(To MISS LUST)
Miss Lust? May I help? Otherwise I shall go mad with boredom.

MISS LUST
I understand. Many of my clients turned to sex for the same reason: boredom. They had nothing better to do than indulge their fantasies, which they quickly wore out. Then came the real problems.
Yes, you may help me with my orchard. It will give your daily schedule some backbone. Everyone should have a garden – or an orchard.

DANIEL
At last! Someone who understands!

MISS LUST
But your fathers. They both understand, now. They have seen as much as anyone under the sun, except Godot. And he is not exactly under the sun.

DANIEL
Oh, Miss Lust...
(He bursts into tears)

MISS LUST
It is all right. You are young. If you are lucky, you will grow old.

B
Let us not be premature.

MISS LUST
(Ignoring B)
There! Now, crying helps. It always does. There...
(DANIEL blows his nose)

MISS LUST
Yes, you are honest with your feelings, and you are honest with yourself. That is good.

DANIEL
Miss Lust, may I marry you?

MISS LUST
What a nice proposal! But if I accepted, everyone else would object. Let us therefore marry. We can work as a team. In fact, most people do try to work as a team, at one point or another. We shall be extending ourselves to them. I do not think Godot would object. After all, he and I were once united, in fact even more than once. Yes, Daniel, I am prepared.
(She pulls out a ring, two rings, and hands one to DANIEL)

Watch out, Mr. Peach is the jealous type.

MR. PEACH
Nonsense. I am through with lust as well as money. I have had enough of snares. Once there was only one red rose in my life. Now, there are many.

MISS LUST
Mr. Peach, you are a marvel.
(MR. PEACH blushes and nods)

MISS LUST
(Continued)
Mr. Peach, we all love you.
(All the characters in the play appear onstage, except GODOT)
(They sing Happy Birthday)

MR. PEACH
But it is not my birthday.

MISS LUST
Every day is a birthday for one of your red roses.
(They all smile)
(Enter GODOT from above, on a swing)

GODOT
Mr. Peach, you are now married to the Goddess of Love, metaphorically speaking. You could not have chosen more fruitfully, or more wisely. Generosity is your creed, love your object, and a red rose is your method. Mr. Peach, you may have whatever in life you may wish.

MR. PEACH
One wish?

GODOT
Yes.

MISS LUST

I would wish for my old job back.

>> DANIEL

I would like my youth over again.

>> B

You are hardly grown up!

>> A

Shhh!

>> B

Well, I would wish to be rid of my headaches,

>> MR. PEACH

I wish that everyone, everywhere have a happy life.
(General astonishment)

>> B

What about you?

>> MR. PEACH

I have told you what I wish. And that is what will make me happy.

>> B

You're a marvel.

>> GODOT

I was not expecting such generosity, Mr. Peach. I am, well, I am surprised. After all, it is I who take the blame for catastrophes, death, disease, and dismemberment. No one has ever wished me well without ulterior motive, even when times were good and omens favorable. In fact, that is when people tend to forget me.

>> MR. PEACH

They couldn't say, "Thank you," could they?

>> GODOT

Yes.

MR. PEACH
Well, I am saying "thank you" for all of us. If you give me my wish, you should have in return what we all believe to be the most wonderful gift of all – love. You have given us life. We are trying to return the favor. No one should be without love, even you. Be kind to us, Mr. Godot. Accept our wish. It is universal.

GODOT
(Tears in eyes)
I shall. I cannot – I do not know what to say.

MISS LUST
Mr. Godot, try "thank you".

GODOT
(To all)
Thank you, thank you all. I suppose I have been preoccupied with everyone's affairs but my own. If I am to live amongst you, then I must indeed love.

MISS LUST
Righto. And we are all here to help. Even Mr. Tops is available.

GODOT
Bring him in!
(All smile)

TOPS
Mr. Godot, you are reputed to be a fast learner.

GODOT
Miss Lust was fast. I just tried to keep up.

TOPS
Please come with me.
(They exit for about two minutes, then reappear)

MISS LUST

Mr. Godot, I hope you take more time when the opportunity presents itself.

TOPS

Oh, he just used the techniques you taught him, with a few minor changes of emphasis. He is ready.

(MISS LUST nods and a splendid YOUNG MAN appears. Lights dim with spots on MISS LUST, MR. TOPS, GODOT and YOUNG MAN)

(Spot on GODOT, then BLACKOUT)

SCENE 16

GODOT
Dessert is such an anti-climax.

YOUNG MAN
You mean climax. We are not physicists. Physicists talk of anti-matter. It is our role in life to discuss what really matters, and it is not anti-matter, or anti-climax.

GODOT
Don't tell me after all I've been through that I'm stuck with a beauty who has a brain.

YOUNG MAN
You said it, not me.

GODOT
Would you care for some psychological testing?

YOUNG MAN
You have been quite adequate. I hope you give me a good report card.

GODOT
I do, I do. Only the clinical psychologists –

YOUNG MAN
Flush them down the drain. Their PhD's will not help them when they first encounter life. And you do not need a PhD to judge me. It is most likely a hindrance. I have never known your judgement to be wrong.

GODOT
I am disarmed!
(They laugh together)

GODOT
(Continued)
We are as well matched as A and B.

YOUNG MAN
Do you think we'll last 2,000 years?

GODOT
I never made predictions, and my expectations are always disappointed.

YOUNG MAN
So are mine. Let us therefore live for the present.

GODOT
Indeed.
(They kiss)

YOUNG MAN
We are scandalous.

GODOT
We need an audience. True love is invariably a scandal.

YOUNG MAN
I thought you were sexually ambiguous.

GODOT
Whatever suits at the time. I try not to force myself into each passing uniform.

YOUNG MAN
Let's try one on.
(They remove themselves upstage)
(A and B enter)

A
What a yucky atmosphere. I am sure there are voyeurs present.
(They look around)

B
Look! A couple, copulating!

A
We are not going to watch.

B
It might be educational.

A
Hey!

B
Ok, ok. I guess it's just as well not to try everything. We might learn more than is good for us.

A
Right.

B
Is there an echo here?

A
Right.

B
Cut it out.

A
Right.

B
I'm sorry, but I was intrigued by that couple.

A
It might derail our relationship. We spent 18 years with Mr. Tops – and lost Daniel. It seems foolish to throw all that wonderful experience out the window.

B
Now I know why we are still together: you have good sense.

A
You do, too. Only you like to indulge yourself.
(GODOT and YOUTH return)

GODOT
We have visitors!

YOUNG MAN
I am the youth.

A
Enchanted.

B
The same. I hope you did not notice us.

YOUNG MAN
It is all right. There is a little of the exhibitionist in all of us. I hope we were not dull.

B
Well, we didn't really look. A was not in favor of it. And I came around to his point of view.

YOUNG MAN
Then we can be real friends, not just porno stars.

A
Of course. That is what we were hoping.

GODOT
I have never been a star of any kind.

YOUNG MAN
Now don't get glorious.

GODOT
I'm not allowed to twinkle?

B
Is that what you call it?

      A
If you want to twinkle, do it for a psychologist, not us.
(Enter PROF. FISH)

      PROF. FISH
I am a clinical psychologist.

      B
Where did you find the time for that?

      PROF. FISH
While fishing.

      GODOT
I shall keep you in mind.

      PROF. FISH
At your service.
(He exits)

      B
If you need a money manager –

      GODOT
Me?????

      B
Oops.

      A
Oops.

      YOUNG MAN
A lawyer might prove useful. I hear a lot of libelous nonsense about you.

      GODOT
(To A and B)
I thought we had covered the topic of religion.

B
It's an occupational hazard.

GODOT
I can live with it.

YOUNG MAN
Wait till they find out about me!

GODOT
What am I supposed to do? Spend all my time talking to heads of stage, witty aristocrats and people of accomplishment? I know I would wear out my welcome very quickly. People like that are not usually fond of criticism, and I am not fond of lies. I prefer to leave them alone. It may teach them something.
(He looks around at everyone)
Meanwhile, we all have each other, as well as the prospect of further acquaintance.

A
That is enough.

B
Yup.

YOUNG MAN
You're all wonders.

GODOT
So are you. I hope it will last.

YOUNG MAN
You are the guide – to eternity.

GODOT
Let's not be extravagant.

YOUNG MAN
Right. Well, let us follow the present forward, and we shall see what we shall see.

                    GODOT
　　Agreed.

                      A
　　Agreed.

                      B
　　Agreed.
(LIGHTS DIM)

SCENE 17

> GODOT
> Are you digging a grave?
>
> B
> This is the resting place of our desires.
>
> A
> Our hopes.
>
> B
> For mankind.
>
> GODOT
> Don't humans have their own hopes?
>
> A
> You mean we're not responsible for everybody?
>
> B
> Each individual can figure out his desires for himself?
>
> GODOT
> It would help.
>
> B
> Everyone wants to make those he knows as like himself as possible.
>
> GODOT
> Look at what the religious have done.
>
> B
> Where is Yorick's skull?
>
> A
> Near the Outer Hebrides?

    B
We must move to Denmark.

    A
Why don't we save that for our next holiday.
(B looks discouraged)
(Enter POTENTATE, disguised as Hamlet)

    A
Who are you?

    POTENTATE
A potentate, disguised as Hamlet.

    A
You are giving yourself away!

    POTENTATE
Only my disguise, not my self. That is what a disguise is for. You give it away, and it comes right back as the latest fashion. I am always on show.

    B
You get used to it.
(They look at the audience)

    POTENTATE
I was not born yesterday.

    B
Evidently.

    A
What's next?

    POTENTATE
Potentates are meant to wield power, but I find the results more satisfactory if I share power with my subjects; so, I have assumed, in my eminence, only a consultative role. Action I leave to actors.

A
So we see.

POTENTATE
What is your problem?

A
B and I have solved that one already. Mr. Tops gave us some pointers. But our son is a royal pain in the butt. And we are afraid he will never find a sensible style of life.

POTENTATE
What is his diet?

A
I don't know.

POTENTATE
You see! What we eat is what we are.

B
What you read is what you are.

POTENTATE
(Ignoring B)
If he is not eating properly, he can be open to all sorts of ill-humor. Does he exercise?

B
Only his tongue.

POTENTATE
You see! Our bodies can sabotage the brain, especially if the brain gets no rest.

B
Oh.

POTENTATE
You two could probably use a few laps around Hyde Park.

                B
Ohh.
                A
Ohh.
            POTENTATE
Well, let us see to your son first…
(Exit A, B, and POTENTATE)
            GODOT
Some potentate.
(TOFF 2 enters)
            TOFF 2
I saw someone going off in the regalia of an Ottoman Emperor.

            GODOT
It's Hamlet. He's preparing for a costume ball.

            TOFF 2
I once went to one. It turned into an orgy.

            GODOT
What did you do?

            TOFF 2
I left. It was a health hazard.
(Pause)

            TOFF 2
(Continued)
I did like the costumes. I went as one of Wellington's aides-decamp. It was a treat.

            GODOT
I would not have been allowed to take sides. Perhaps I could have participated as an experienced intermediary. I've always wanted to dress up. In the few places I go these days, it is necessary to dress down.

TOFF 2
I shall see what I can find in the way of fancy military dress.

GODOT
Thank you.
(TOFF 2 exits)
(TOFF 2 then re-enters with a costume)

GODOT
Oh! This is splendid.

TOFF 2
Try it on.
(GODOT does so)

GODOT
Oh – I feel enthralling.

TOFF 2
The women will love you.

GODOT
They already do,

TOFF 2
Then they will love you some more.

GODOT
Don't tease.

TOFF 2
I'm serious.

GODOT
This is fun.

TOFF 2
You see.

GODOT
Yes.

TOFF 2
What a lesson.

GODOT
Yes.

TOFF 2
Where is the Potentate?
(Voice offstage)

POTENTATE
Coming!
(Enter POTENTATE with DANIEL)

DANIEL
I must have hurt them very early on.

POTENTATE
It is B that is hurt – and still is.

DANIEL
What can I do?

POTENTATE
Do you love him?

DANIEL
I love them both.

POTENTATE
So please be demonstrative. Cut the crap and treat them as they deserve. You are their future. They can help you survive.

DANIEL
You are too much.
(He starts crying)

POTENTATE
(Holding DANIEL)
You have a big heart.

DANIEL
So do A and B.
(He cries some more)

POTENTATE
Well. Let's not spend the day prone. Up and at 'em.
(They both get up)

TOFF 2
(To GODOT, who nods)
Ready? Everyone in costume. Present yourselves.
(A and B enter tgether dressed as harlequins)
(DANIEL appears as Howdy Doody)

B
(To A, pointing to DANIEL)
It's him. Don't say anything and he won't find out who we are.

A
B!

B
Watch.
(He walks up to Howdy Doody and, disguising his voice, speaks)

B
I am the Ace of Spades.

DANIEL
Nonsense.
(He laughs)
You are B. And there is A.

B
(His balloon punctured)
How did you know?

DANIEL
Body language. Mr. Tops taught me.

B
But you never studied with Mr. Tops.

DANIEL
I studied with you, incognito.

A
It is called being a child.

B
It is called being a faithful son.
(He embraces DANIEL)

POTENTATE
Let everyone keep the faith!
(At this point, the whole cast emerge onstage dressed for a ball. And that is what they have)

A
Ooohh. Well done.
(Lights up to watch the dancing and singing. SLOW FADE)

-FINIS-

www.ingramcontent.com/pod-product-compliance
Lightning Source LLC
Chambersburg PA
CBHW030156100526
44592CB00009B/303